BROKEN FLOWERS
AND OTHER STAIRWAYS TO HEAVEN

OTHER BOOKS BY ROBERT M. DRAKE

SPACESHIP (2012)

SCIENCE (2013)

BEAUTIFUL CHAOS (2014)

BLACK BUTTERFLY (2015)

A BRILLIANT MADNESS (2015)

BEAUTIFUL AND DAMNED (2016)

BROKEN FLOWERS

AND OTHER STAIRWAYS TO HEAVEN

ROBERT
M. DRAKE

Andrews McMeel Publishing
a division of Andrews McMeel Universal
1130 Walnut Street, Kansas City, Missouri 64106

www.andrewsmcmeel.com

17 18 19 20 21 RR2 10 9 8 7 6 5 4 3 2

ISBN: 978-1-4494-8630-3

Library of Congress Control Number: 2016951403

Book design: Robert M. Drake

First Edition 2016

Contact: RMDRKONE@gmail.com

ATTENTION: SCHOOLS AND BUSINESSES
Andrews McMeel books are available at quantity discounts with bulk purchase for educational, business, or sales promotional use. For information, please e-mail the Andrews McMeel Publishing Special Sales Department: specialsales@amuniversal.com.

For Sevyn and The 9 Street Boys.

This one is for you.

She will always be a reflection
of all the people she wants to love.

BROKEN FLOWERS

AND OTHER STAIRWAYS TO HEAVEN

Andrews McMeel
PUBLISHING®

I'm still figuring out what this life is worth
and I need you to be with me,
to hold my hand because everything else
is too heavy to hold.

CONTENTS

BROKEN FLOWERS
AND OTHER STAIRWAYS TO HEAVEN

It's raining again on my side
and I can't help but wonder
if you're safe and sound.

I'm sorry for all the storms
I left behind.

BROKEN FLOWERS

AND OTHER STAIRWAYS TO HEAVEN

ROBERT M. DRAKE

I feel too much, I love too much, and
I always give people the best of me,
even when I know they don't deserve it at all.

BROKEN FLOWERS
AND OTHER STAIRWAYS TO HEAVEN

Of all the storms I've watched fly by,
you've been the only one I've chased.

Go On

And you will go on

searching for the best of you

and you will never find it,

but that is the point.

Do not miss the point.

Missing it will make

the beautiful struggle useless.

And believe me you need it.

It is what will make you.

The fact that you will keep

trying to find the perfect you,

the perfect moment

and connection and love.

And you will die trying.

We will all die trying.

But that is the goddamn point.

To never stop searching for

the things that remind you

how to feel, how to live,

and how to die the right way,

your way . . .

The only way to do things.

Do Not Run from Yourself

You can run all you want

but one day

someone is going to take

ahold of you, kid,

and find you

and maybe they will even

run with you.

And who knows.

Maybe they will stick around

for longer than usual

and make things harder

to run away from.

We are all running away

or toward something, kid.

Let us just hope whatever

it is we crash into does not

make the day dimmer

and the night darker.

You deserve at least

ten thousand suns.

We all do.

When My Brother Left

Brother,

I remember when you told me

you felt different

and at that moment

I couldn't understand why.

A few years later

and now I, too, feel different,

like the first time I heard that one song—

the one that changed my life.

I now understand

what you were going through.

I get it.

I met a girl on a train

and now I feel different about

almost everything,

and I want to go back to the way

things were, but things

are not that easy when you are

in love.

Things just never look the same.

I Miss You

You seemed fine

the last time we spoke.

You seemed better,

as if somewhere in this

endless dark space

you found a map,

and it led you

out of this world.

I hope you find what

you're looking for.

I hope you come back soon.

Sometimes I drown things, people,
and memories. Sometimes I rise
to the surface and kiss the shore
and sometimes you are the ocean.

Tonight It Is Good

Life is harder when you

see it for what it is,

for what it can be.

From bad to worse,

from worse to better.

And the night becomes day,

and the pain becomes less

than what it was

the night before.

Tonight it is all good.

The company is all good

and none of us worry about

the morning sun.

Tonight all the people have

a flower somewhere inside

of them, and they are looking

for somewhere to bloom.

Somewhere to be themselves

in the middle of the night.

What Is Important

What you consider important right now

might change within the next moment.

You could never be content

considering everything is always changing

and growing.

The same with people.

They are always changing and growing.

You have to learn how to change

and grow with them

if you ever want a shot at someone to love.

Even if that means leaving

the things you are familiar with

behind.

I do not know how it began
but I do remember how it ended,
and I will find you in the
endless days of summer because
that was where I fell into you.

I Wish I Saw You

I'm losing parts of myself

that I haven't found yet,

and I can feel them

walking in and out of me.

Some never return

and some come back,

just to fuck with me.

You know that feeling?

Two people slowly becoming strangers,

slowly burning till there's nothing left?

That's what this is like

and I think I'm okay with that.

Maybe in some distant future,

in another place,

or even in another earth,

you and I could be more

than just people we used to know.

What You Became

You are all

the old records I listen to.

You are the books I read,

all the places I visit,

and all the poetry I have yet to write.

My dearest friend . . .

You are the forgiveness

I need to give myself

for not being there for you.

You are more than these

words and these feelings

you have left behind.

You are light,

and the light contained inside of you,

it is beyond belief,

the theory of everything.

It is raining again on my side
and I cannot help but wonder
if you are safe and sound. I am
sorry for all the storms I left
behind.

What Some People Bring

Someone will always

be watching you.

Someone will always be

out to get you,

no matter where you go.

You cannot run far enough

from the bullshit

people bring.

You will find people

like this everywhere.

They are so damn sad

about their own lives

that they feel the need

to bring others down.

You go on . . .

Someone will always be

there, you will see,

and you must, for the goodness

of your own life . . .

Watch back with eyes

like the moon and blood

in your hands.

Watch back and wait

for one of them to make

their move.

Where You Can Find Me

And I will wait for you

under the soft rain.

I will wait for you

in the empty bottles of wine,

in the ripped sky,

and in the moments

where I picked myself up.

I will wait for you

where I first met you.

I will wait for you here,

because this was the place

where we saw each other

for the last time.

We Get It

Yeah you are real, we get it.

You remind the crowd around you

every five minutes.

You talk about

how much alcohol you drink,

every five minutes.

You talk about

how many women you sleep with,

every five minutes.

You talk about this and that,

things that you think appeal to the crowd.

We get it! We get it! God, we get it!

You are as real as they come,

but you know what type of person

does not have to say they are

"a real motherfucker"?

A REAL motherfucker.

Glory

You only go to that place

when you feel like

you don't fit in,

when you think people

do not understand you.

You only go to that place

when you want to be alone

because you think

the world wants to rob you

of your glory.

But that might not be the case.

That might not even be

what you need.

So do not go there,

that place is not for you.

Do not go away, you might

lose yourself in there

and you might never find

your way back.

The Sun Wants to Come In

You never really see

how bad it can get

until you become

a part of the problem

and it usually happens

without us even knowing it.

And most will never know,

that's how it is.

People, almost all are

always quicker

to fall into any problem

at any given moment.

It is almost like they follow

us and they are waiting

for a little sunshine to enter

us through our eyes.

And that is when they strike.

They overflow and dry

the sun out like a lit match

interested in the water.

This dark cloud is easy

to follow, it is hard to escape,

but that is our problem.

And that is one we must

learn to starve on our own.

No One Wants to Stay

Sometimes I feel like

I have been here too long,

maybe even forever.

I feel like I am trapped in this page.

Caged inside myself.

Trapped beneath the ground

looking for the photons

that will lead me out,

that will leak me out,

and keep me out.

No one ever wants to stay

in the same place

or do the same things

for several years.

The years begin to look

the same and everything

that is the same becomes

madness, becomes hysterical,

if you stare long enough.

Now tell me how sad

it is to have so much poetry inside

but not enough pages,

not enough words

to write them down.

That is what this is like,

like all the love I have for you

trapped inside my body.

All the nights I envision you,

together with our hands mangled.

That is what this is like,

like the everything

and the nothing about you

is inside of me

and I do not know what

to do or where to go.

Sometimes I want to show

you more of me,

but I do not know how.

You should talk to strangers
more. You should learn from them
and grow with them. Sometimes
a stranger could save you and
sometimes a smile could change
a life.

Speak to Me

I always found myself

getting into the hardest of situations,

in and out of the worst

moments or so I thought,

but that's how I was. I was reckless.

I was always willing to go

through hell and back

as long as it meant something.

And I was never sure

what it meant to begin with,

but if it spoke to me beyond the words,

beyond the flesh,

then I went for it, in that very moment.

I went for it blindly

whether it was good or bad.

I dove my ambition, my inspiration,

into these rare little moments

like a giant rock

falling from the sky.

Wood Tavern

It's been a while since

I last went out,

perhaps too long,

or long enough for me

to dream of crowds.

Sometimes you just have to

go out there and experience

life a little. You can't always stay

in and expect to learn

something new about people

from reading goddamn books.

Human understanding

does not work that way.

I go into Wood Tavern one night

and of course it is a rare thing

for me to see this haven empty.

"There are too many people," I thought.

Too many faces and they are waiting

for something—like a spaceship.

Something to come out of the sky

and tell them how beautiful they are.

And they are, every single one of them.

It felt good to be out.

I walked to the bar

and I got a drink spilled on me.

This is how good turns bad.

The girl turns around and says

"Sorry," then turns back around

and goes on with her night.

Now my shirt was wet, but

I went on with my night too.

I drank, I laughed, and I forgot

how I left.

When I got home I sat in front of the

old typewriter and wrote this here prose

you are reading right now . . .

I typed and thought,

I thought and typed

and I still do not understand

humans at all, including myself.

"There are lights in the sky,"
said the little girl.
"Those are not lights, dear,
those are people," said her
father.

You Are My Air

I hope you see things

differently now,

and I hope you know

we did not destroy ourselves

when we thought our

worlds had ended.

Because we are still here

and we still exist

because the other still lives.

You are my air

and I am your lungs.

I Want to Save You

I told you I wanted to

save the world,

to do something about

all this pain.

You told me how that

was impossible and how

I am only one person.

Nothing is impossible.

It takes one sun to light the sky,

one moon to move the tide,

and one love to change a life.

I love you.

I will change you.

I will save us all.

Closer Than We Think

I feel the same way.

You feel the same way.

Everyone feels the same way.

And we just do not know

how to tell each other.

We just want a way

out of our own humanity,

out of our own skin.

Because the world has made us believe

we are not beautiful,

we are not capable

of becoming art.

But I see you walking.

I see the paint falling off

your shoes as if

I see Van Gogh,

Michelangelo, and Da Vinci

pouring out of the way

you move.

You are beautiful,

and the world wants to

mutilate your story.

It wants to erase the words

so we all think the same.

So we all think less.

I need you to know you are

more. You have to see it.

Open your eyes.

The child in you did not die.
The child in you is alive
and it is waiting to show you
the world in a different light.

Before It Began

And just like that,

before it even began

it was over.

The moment I thought

I belonged,

I found myself

back where I started.

And I thought:

"How in the hell could

anyone keep their sanity

playing this game?"

And that answer was simple:

"We were all willing to

die a little for a chance

to be loved."

The Love in You

But you have to find the

place that brings out

the human in you.

The soul in you.

The love in you.

You have to sing a little

in there.

You do not have to do it

all the time,

but at least every once

in a while.

Anything beats the silence.

Anything beats

the quietness of the clock

when you are missing

the company of another

person.

If your breath tells your story
then let it flow with the wind.
Let it touch the sky and make
love to the moon. I want to feel
you everywhere I go.

When You Cross My Mind

Sometimes

I think of you,

and sometimes

I wonder if you made it

out of your life alive.

I know it is not safe

to stay within yourself.

For almost all

who have ever found

something deep enough

to stir them,

have found it out

of their goddamn

normal lives.

And I am still here,

looking for you

on the other side.

Strange Beautiful Girl

There is something

strange about your beauty.

The way your eyes clash,

they make me feel

as if you are from

another time,

perhaps even

another planet,

another moment.

One that defeats what I am,

and one that defines me

to the raw bone.

What I am trying to say is,

you break me down

in ways I could have

never imagined.

No matter how far you go,
I will always be near. I will
always be with you, even when
you feel alone.

We Can Still Fly

There will always be

parts of me that only you

can unlock,

that only you can

come back to save,

and that only you can

calm, too soon.

What remains of me,

will always fill

the emptiness in you.

It will always complete

all that we have.

The only parts

we have not learned

to say good-bye to.

The only parts

where we

can still be free.

I Will Return

And if you ever came back

then I'd promise

to give you the raw truth,

and how it was all about

me when I left you.

You weren't ready,

and I wasn't either.

I was somewhere else.

I was looking for ways

to better myself, to heal.

And you were stuck

on the past, believing

it would somehow save

us from our future.

I couldn't give in.

I'm sorry. I am better

than that.

I made myself from all the love
you never gave me, from all the
attention I never received.
I am strong now and I do not need
you.

Tigers and Women

Some women are more

dangerous than tigers,

and having at least one

on your side might be

the smartest thing

a man can do.

But treat them well,

for all things change overnight.

If you push them a little

they can become something else,

something like a killer

and their genius is enough

to send a man into suicide,

into hell.

It is true . . .

A woman can turn a man

against himself

and there is nothing more

deadly than that.

The Freedom You Deserve

I'd like to believe

that maybe somewhere,

out there, in the vast darkness,

you have finally found

that freedom you would

always talk about.

And I'd like to believe

that you are a bird

and I am the wind

that pushes you

toward the sun.

And that maybe

the light in you did not

burn out, that maybe

it just left for a little while

and that maybe one day

it will soon find its

way back home.

Believe in people and you will grow in all the places they never thought you would.

I Don't Know You Anymore

We are all fighting

to be ourselves

in a world that tells us

who we should be.

And it makes me wonder

if I am in love

with the real you

or just the person you

think you are.

What We Have Inside

Sitting here,

next to you,

I have come

to the conclusion

how it is all the same.

From stars to people,

we are all

drowning

in a pool

filled with too much

to handle.

Too much stress.

Too much fear.

It rises like the vapor

that escapes from our

lungs and bursts into

nothing, into air.

It is all the same,

and it all ends the same.

From stars to people.

We die within ourselves,

waiting for whatever it is

our souls are made of

to claim us and soften

us up to drift away

into the sky.

Sitting here,

next to you,

I have come to the

conclusion,

how it is all the same.

From stars to people,

we are all

struggling with parts

of ourselves

we are too afraid

to reveal.

Feel It in Your Lungs

Look up at the sky.

This must be the sign.

The one we look for

to get away.

The one we look for

when such sad things happen.

If there is something you

have been waiting for,

then this is it.

You feel that air filling your lungs?

That is it . . .

Today . . .

can still be yours.

Sadness is an ocean and sometimes
I drown while other times I have
no choice but to swim.

Then There Is You

What you gave me

only happens once

and it is not meant

to come back again.

So if I must put it into words

then I must admit,

how not all good things are good

and not all bad things are bad.

And then there is you

and you really fucked me over,

but it felt good,

at least good enough.

And I cannot understand why,

but you still pull out the laughter

in me.

You are in my head

when no one else is around.

It Slip through Your Hands

You took someone

that understood you:

a lover or a friend.

And you watched them

become the only thing

worth clinging to

in the brokenness of the world.

And then, it ends,

as all things end,

suddenly and fast.

Like one day you are

shaped by their laughter,

and then the next day,

eaten alive by their memory.

I can't understand it at all.

You build yourself with

someone you love

and in an instant they are gone.

It ends,

and all you are left with

is

the bitterness

that made sense

in the company

of what

once was.

Love will always be one of those

things, and it will always hurt

a little more than the last time.

You cannot get away from it

and

that is all

that is needed

to say

about that.

Do What You Must

Anything could happen here.

Maybe you will find someone

and fall in love.

But of course,

just like everyone else,

you keep spending most of your time

looking.

And you have been looking

hard enough, so hard

that when it finally arrives,

you barely remember what it was

you were looking for

and

when it comes to you

it usually arrives beyond the expectation.

And you,

like the person you never knew,

ignore it.

It comes close enough,

and it is all too fast to hold.

And then you,

like the person you never knew,

you do nothing,

you say nothing,

and think nothing . . .

as you watch the love of your life

pass you by.

I break things. That is the only
thing I know how to do. And
sometimes you break me and because
of it, I love you.

I Remember You

You look different now,

like someone else

and you sound

like someone else too.

And I can barely recognize you anymore.

But there is something

familiar inside of you,

that chaos,

that same wild energy

that I have.

And tonight I see it piercing

out of you,

and it is calling my name,

the same way mine called yours

many moons ago,

like the night I betrayed myself

and fell fast

into love.

I Miss You Again

If I told you

I did not miss you

then I am a liar.

I miss you.

I miss you.

I miss you.

But you have become

another stranger,

someone I used to know.

Another sunset

with no other place

to go.

Break me by the rocks and leave me there. Let me come back to you on the shore. Let me become all the seashells you were meant to collect.

Give Yourself a Chance

Too many faces,

too many places,

many things within many things

and in so many ways

they could all inspire your life,

if only

you gave them all

a chance.

Dualism

There is a sun to your moon.

A soul to your body.

A yes to your no.

You are alive while you are dying.

Sleeping while you are awake.

There is a god to your devil.

A dream to your nightmare.

It can go on. It will always go on.

There is a forever to your end.

A friend to your stranger.

A movement to your stillness.

A hello to your last good-bye.

A yesterday to your today.

A past to your present.

A wholeness to your emptiness.

A love to your hate.

A something to your nothing.

But most of all,

there is a happiness to your sadness.

And if you ever lose it, just remember,

soon enough it will find you

and the ride back

will be the most precious thing

known to your earth.

This Mad Cycle

And like everything

that matters—it goes on,

and then it is ignored,

and then it is left to be forgotten.

And it never stops,

this cycle,

this endless war

of attention and appreciation.

It greets no end.

It is all taken from

the people we see every day,

the places,

and all things that pass us by.

It is all taken for granted, eventually.

It all goes on.

What to Do if I Break

Catch me now

as I break

into a million pieces.

Into the air,

into the ocean,

and into all the fiery regions

where people like us

fight for a chance

to be loved.

Let me put it like this: In one hundred years we will all be dead. So why not express what we feel while we are still here.

Rooms and Memory

I am here

because you

made me up in your head.

I am here

because it is easier

to echo through the rooms

in your mind

than the rooms we try

to each other in at night.

I am here.

I am all around you,

inside, staying.

I am in your head.

Keep me in there

and I will always be around.

I will always be near,

even when you feel

like you need to get away.

Real Is Real

What is wrong with the world?

We used to hate racism, violence,

poverty, famine, and more.

Now everyone hates on anything,

anytime they get the chance to.

The music you listen to.

The films you watch.

The books you read.

The clothes you wear

and the way you speak.

They even hate you in your own skin.

If you tripped over,

they would even hate on

the way you fell.

The real of the real is . . .

how people do not know

what to hate on anymore.

They have all run out of things to destroy.

I do not know why people hurt but
I do know one thing: Silence heals
everything and I have enough of
it to save the world.

Unravel

Unravel this skin, what it is

that holds me together,

what it is that contains all the pieces of me.

Unravel me, save me, and set me free

in the silence of all things that go on to be

ignored.

Unravel me, in the train, on a Sunday afternoon,

in the middle of the rain,

or when there is nothing left to do.

Unravel me and find me,

beneath the skin, where the chaos that

makes me is beautiful.

Unravel me to understand me.

I will wait there. I will rest there.

And you will learn to love me there.

A Bird Flew Through

I'd like to believe that

somewhere out there

someone has done the right

thing with you.

I'd like to believe

that someone has made you laugh

in the middle of the night,

that someone has left the sun

in your pocket, in your hair, and

in those little moments where

you feel free.

I'd like to believe that

you are flying within yourself

because there is a paradise in you.

There is so much more.

And

I hope you are doing well,

even if it is not with me.

You should follow your heart.
It does not always get you into
trouble, for sometimes the heart
finds what the eye cannot see,
and believe me, there is so much
of it around you.

And Here We Are

And here we are . . .

two people pretending to be

people we are not,

two people wanting to be more.

So when we tell other people

we used to know each other,

it's just us saying:

We once knew people

we could have been,

and

maybe when all of this

suffering is over I'll see you

again and build something

real and be happy there.

I Built Cathedrals out of You

I know I do not

know you anymore

but

you still remind me

of what it was like

to be here,

to be in peace.

You will always be

the best parts to all

the forgotten places

I used to love.

What We Are

It is not about the places

you have seen

or the things you own.

It is about the people

you have met and the way

they made you feel.

So pick and choose.

You do not need all of them

to make it through the day,

just a few,

and there are always a few

good people coming in

and out of your life.

So please do not be afraid.

Keep their trust.

Their friendship is important.

Another Earth

I am not from this earth.

I cannot cope with the ways

of the world:

It is too damn hard.

Where I am from,

there are no photos to scroll,

no videos to watch,

no small bright screens,

and no buttons to type

what I am thinking.

Where I am from,

we wonder what people

are up to, go see them,

and sit outside with them

for hours.

I do not know where it

went wrong and I do not know

how to fix it.

What I am trying to say is,

I miss the old you,

the real you,

and I want to forget

what we have become,

what this world has become.

And I hope we see each other soon.

I have so much to tell you.

There is darkness trapped in your
rib cage and there is also light.
What you do with the two is up to
you. I just hope you do not confuse
the two. The world needs night
and day to function and so do you.

Go Outside

When someone smiles at you

for no reason.

When you are inside a room

filled with people you love.

When a miracle happens.

When your best friend says good-bye.

When you leave that city that changed your life.

When you're on a train and you fall in love

with a stranger.

When you pluck a flower

and ignore it has a few hours to live.

When you lie in your bed

and think about the night before.

When you take a photo with someone

you will never see again.

When your heart is broken

and slowly heals itself.

When you lose yourself in the chaos

of the world . . .

to find yourself in the end.

This is where you hurt the most.

This is where you live the most.

In the moments that give you breath,

and in the moments that take it away.

Filled In-boxes

"R. M. Drake, your work is too long now. I liked
you better when you wrote short things for me to
read."

"R. M. Drake, you have changed. Your style is too
different and difficult to swallow now."

"R. M. Drake, I miss the old you. You used to be so
much better."

These are the kind of messages I get now.

Hell, I guess I'm not supposed to grow and evolve.

I guess I am supposed to be inhuman and not learn a

thing as time goes on.

Silly humans must learn.

If you are not changing then you are not growing

and if you are not growing then there is no chance

of survival.

Surviving is the rebellion against oneself. It is

the change that happens even if we do not want it

to arrive ourselves.

Wild girl with wild hair, I see you and I know what you are up to. You want the world and everything in it and there is nothing anyone could do to stop you. Just remember a tamed woman will never leave her mark on the world. Stay wild.

Real Talk

'Cause love is real

and talk is cheap

and you had enough words

to bring down

the whole goddamn city.

And I, like the fool,

believed in them

and that is probably

the only thing real between us.

You got me

and I got words

and every single one of them

drunk in the lie of love.

And it is not enough to say

you fucked me over.

You fucked me over like

all lovers who get fucked over.

They take it all in . . .

and exhale, while trying to figure out

where all the love is really

meant to go.

Violent Power

Power and violence,

now they must go hand in hand.

But c'mon no one ever talks about it

and when they do,

people act like they know about it,

but the truth is,

nobody knows anything about it.

Not even the ones starting

the goddamn wars know

anything about it.

And there they go wanting more power

and then think they will gain it

by killing each other.

But that is not true power.

There is no true force in violence.

The times are changing.

If any of you reading this wants power,

then inspire someone with all heart

and do not pretend. Go in all the way.

Believe in their goodness,

believe,

the same way a child would believe.

Even the worst of wars are won

by those who believe in something

greater than themselves.

The Generation

I cannot help but wonder

how some people

have the power to do anything in the world:

save it, cure it, and change it,

but go on to destroy it themselves.

They destroy it as if it is the only thing they can

do.

This generation has it all wrong.

They use fear to lead

and violence to control.

They are fed lies

and do not know what to believe

in anymore.

They do not know each other

and they do not know where to go.

This Reality

We are in fact a part

of this prison but often

my comrades and I would say,

if ever we were to escape

this reality, this prison,

we would find ourselves

in a bigger prison, in a bigger reality, and so on

and so forth.

So even if we wanted to,

we could never be free,

for there will always be

something bigger,

something better,

and something harder

to run away from . . .

Just like you . . .

there will always be a bigger

and better person

within the person,

of the person that you are.

The Sun Is Like You

And everything seems

to feel better

when you are around,

and now I see this light

and it kind of lets me see

where I am going.

I now know where I have to go.

I will tell you when I get there.

I will send mail to you

with all the little things

that will remind me of you.

We go to places to seek
adventure, to find ourselves.
Well, I say, I go to places
to find things that remind me
of you.

For Gui

And all I want is to bring you back from the dead,

my brother.

And all I want is to tell your mother how

everything will be okay.

And all I want is to wake up and let this all be

some kind of terrible joke.

And all I want is to forget that last time I told

you good-bye.

And all I want is one more day with you, for I know

I could have saved you from that last night you

spent on earth.

And all I want is to tell you I am sorry for not being

a friend.

I'm sorry. I'm sorry. I'm sorry.

That is all I truly want.

Be You

I need you to be you,

and that is all I want.

I want you to become

the person you want to become.

Not for your friends

or family

or for the new promises

you make to yourself every year.

Become who you want

to become for the person

inside of you.

The one you let out

when no one is around.

That is the real you.

That is who you should be.

That is who I want to meet,

and that is who I want to love.

Those sparks you see coming out
of me are my thoughts and feelings
and sometimes they are all about
you.

The Last

The last conversation was always the worst. This is

something I have always thought.

But I ran into her a few years later. And I

discovered that the last conversation isn't the

worst. It is the one you have the next time you

meet, accidentally of course.

"Why did you help find me if all you wanted to do

was leave me behind?

"Why did you love me if in the end you left all this

pain behind?"

I had nothing to say . . .

"I don't hate you. I don't hate anyone really."

Shocked at the questions she was asking. She didn't even care to bother how I was doing. Women are like that at times. They don't forget, so please watch out with them.

"I just want to understand what it is like to be an asshole, that is all," she said.

The words did not pour, and that was unusual. The words always pour.

Sometimes you are the asshole everyone warns you about even

if you cannot see it for yourself.

Raindrops

You said I was the rain

for the way I fell

and I said you were a river

for the way you ran.

The way you ran from the pain

the whole goddamn world

had caused you.

And now, you are gone . . .

And now, all I have left

are the things I have

to make myself from:

from all the things

that are no longer here.

From the shatter in your eyes,

to what it is like to fall forever.

From all the things that used to matter,

to all the things that made me feel.

So keep running my friend, keep finding . . .

and I will do my best with falling

and finding as well.

Allow yourself to be picked.
Allow yourself to break.
Allow yourself to hurt.
Open yourself to all these things
and you will appreciate everything
most people tend to ignore.

What I Didn't Learn about You

And now

I set you free

among the wolves.

So please go,

go now,

go find them,

and kill them softly

with all the things

this earth has

never revealed to you.

Kill them all

with the love

you never had.

The Message I Wrote for Myself

And there was

nothing left to hurt . . .

That's how I knew

it was over.

And in the end,

I belonged to myself,

and I was finally able

to change—for me.

The love I had inside me

didn't belong to you

or anyone I ever knew . . .

It was all, ultimately,

meant for me.

Say Something

I know you want to

say something.

I know you want to

save me, understand me,

but for some odd reason

the people that don't

know me, are the people

who really understand me.

They are the ones

who will help me save myself.

So yes, the world is

a terrible place.

You don't need to explain it any further.

I get it, believe me, I really do.

But sometimes it takes

a complete stranger

to help you realize

how you have the power

to get up, and put yourself

back together again.

Knowing All Is Knowing Nothing

They say I have to know you to love you.

You have to tell me things like

your favorite colors,

what kind of films you watch,

and what kind of music

you listen to, etc.

And then, possibly,

after knowing all those things about you,

I am supposed to see

if we are compatible with each other,

that is, if we have enough things

in common.

Well, I do not abide by those rules

and right now, I only want to know

what is in your mind,

all the things you are too afraid to say,

the rain you have within.

I want to know everything

that hurts and I only want to

love everything that is unreachable.

Do not become like other people.
People are full of shit and they
are mostly wrong. Trust yourself.
Only you know how to fill your
lungs with breath. Only you know
who you are.

Deserve to Love

And I hope you find

more than just yourself.

I hope you find

the strength

not to hurt the people

who love you.

I hope you find

a thousand miracles

hidden in the soft rain.

And I hope you find art

in all the people

you deserve to love.

Colors Change

I don't expect you

to be the same because

a lot has changed.

I mean, I'm not the same

person you remember me as.

I'm better, a lot better.

So to be real with you

I'm not interested

in the small talk, although

I do have a lot to get off my chest

on how careless you were

back then, but to be honest

I don't even care anymore

and that's the reality.

So let that sink in for a while,

let that burn, let that eat the flesh,

because the truth is,

reality is reality

and sometimes reality knocks

the wind out of you.

I just don't really give a damn

to even witness it.

Miracles

And anything could happen here.

A miracle could happen.

You finding yourself

could happen.

Hell, maybe you

could even find someone

and fall in love . . .

Who knows . . .

All you have to do is believe.

Beautiful things happen

when you begin to believe.

Muse

I found almost everything

about her to be inspiring,

but I also found it

inspiring: how we could

send a man to the moon,

how we could split atoms,

and how we could

communicate halfway

around the world . . .

But there was such a difference

in this newfound inspiration.

It made me feel good

about myself and I found

that to be incredible.

She was like a dream,

and sometimes that's

what we all need.

A dream to help us

get through our daily lives.

A Little Fire

Keep a little fire going,

a little self-love,

and a little confidence.

Keep it hidden in you,

if you must,

but keep it—nonetheless.

Do not let it out

until you feel you must,

until it is the only thing

left to do.

And if it doesn't belong anywhere,

then create a place

where it would.

Let the whole world know

how your greatness started

from just one spark.

Show them why legends

never die.

She Part 3

She didn't know what she wanted

and she knew how no one ever did . . .

But she did know one thing:

She wanted to be found in the rain.

She wanted to run wild . . .

She wanted to fall, and feel safe,

but dangerous enough

to let her heart drop.

She wanted love,

true love, pure and kind and untouched.

The kind that wasn't ruined

by the chaos of the world.

The kind you would find

in a small coffee shop

in some foreign country.

That is all she really wanted,

and she didn't know where

or how it would appear,

but she knew, deep within her,

it would show itself

in the form of something

unexpected.

The Rocks inside You

There is something heavy

inside of you.

Something that is preventing

you from moving on.

I can see it in you.

I can see it in all of us.

We are all connected

by the same sorrow

and the same regret.

Eventually, without reason,

we learn from

their hidden truths.

We learn how a million

different things can go wrong,

and how a million

different things can go right.

Without pain and loss,

there is no perfect nirvana;

only such a place can

exist at the edge of

our doom.

Things I Once Saw

The people were too busy doing little things,

getting by. You know, working the same ol' beat-up

jobs.

Driving the same ol' beat-up cars.

Dreaming the same ol' beat-up dreams.

Waiting for something to free them from the

boredom.

And they wait and they wait.

As they live they wait to either

win the lottery or in some way

save the world.

They wait and then they wait some more . . .

But those who want to win the lottery don't play

enough

to win and those who want

to save the world don't believe

in themselves enough to save it.

They wait with their tired jobs, cars, and dreams.

You have got to take action, believe a little more,

and maybe you might win the lottery.

You might even save the world.

Who knows, keep pushing, just know that there is

something better on the other side.

People think they know people, when really they do not. We were not meant to be understood. We are meant to go and all I see are the footprints you left behind.

Rise

Rise from the clear waters of your soul and bloom

enough to drink the air and wild of the sea.

Drown yourself and be fueled by the fire

that breathes under the water.

Become the light.

Expose yourself to the light for it lives in you,

and I promise you will grow there.

Tell Me the Truth

You should tell people

how you feel.

You should be open and truthful.

You should get up

every time you fall.

You should fight

for what is important.

By that I mean

all the things that keep you

up at night.

You should believe in every breath

that leaves your body.

You are a walking miracle.

You should laugh a little more.

It looks so fucking good on you.

You should do all these things,

but only when you are ready.

Everything will begin,

your world will begin,

but only when you are ready.

People Still Go

And I found myself asking why

certain people never came back.

And I asked myself why

I would always change

when someone would leave.

And I asked my mind,

several times,

why it would replay memories

that I had never lived.

And in the hour of silence,

I did discover one thing—

how everyone deserved

a chance to move on,

and how all was still

and only the people were moving.

Scared of It All

And you tell everyone

how much you have accomplished.

And you tell everyone

how much you are loved.

And you tell everyone

about all the adventures you have had.

And you tell everyone . . .

and tell everyone . . .

and tell everyone everything

about you.

And still,

in the middle of the crowd,

you feel more alone than ever.

You wonder why

eventually they all leave.

Sometimes people are only interested

in things you are too afraid to say.

The String of Your Soul

And every day . . .

let something pull you in.

And every day . . .

let something catch your attention.

And every day . . .

find something new.

And every day . . .

find summer in all winters.

And every day . . .

fly toward the sun.

And every day . . .

feel beautiful (because you are).

And every day . . .

discover how love does not fade.

And every day . . .

find growth: quietly.

Live this way and every day you will

be closer to the perfect version of you.

Every day is important, if only

you gave it and yourself a chance.

And Now

And now they have departments

for everything you own.

For your car,

for your house,

for your kids,

for your money,

for your school,

and even your own dreams.

And they can, if they wanted to,

take it all away. Not even the people you love

belong to you. Death is always waiting in the back

of the show . . . that, and they want you to think

it all belongs to you.

And what a shame it is how nothing is ever really

yours . . .

The only thing you own is your debt

and you carry it with you as if it is pushed by

your skin.

Debt is inevitable . . .

Nothing more.

Nothing less.

The Truth

The truth is never easy

but it should come out of you

like breath, like the life

you hold within.

Speak of it

and one day the love

lost in your eyes

will take you to

another place.

The one that is waiting for you

to be revealed.

I can not recognize my hands.
I do not know what they are made
for, if they are not touching
yours.

In the Middle of the Street

There are some people who come into your life with a light so bright they make you forget where you are. Find these people and live in their suns. You are their planets and you are their moons.

And that is how life is meant to be lived. How people are meant to be loved. Be someone's light, even in the middle of the street.

Something New

And then there are the people

who will buy something new,

go somewhere different,

and even switch crowds

to feel better about themselves.

But what they fail to understand is,

true happiness

doesn't work this way.

You have to find it from within.

So no matter where you go,

what you buy, or who you

spend your time with . . .

your demons will still be with you,

and you have to find a way

to bury them

before they go ahead

and bury you instead.

Do Not Be Like Them

Do not be like them.

Do not be like one of those

sad people who complain

about sad things.

They go on to live sad lives.

Be not like them.

Be different.

Be you.

Be happy.

And you will find the light in you without even

realizing it . . .

That I promise.

They Say

"They say when someone leaves, something inside of

you dies, but

they also say something inside of you is born."

That must have been the line that set me off, that

set off this whole writing gig.

My friend of twenty-plus years called me over the

telephone.

Now, I hate phone calls,

I hate text messages,

and most of the time,

I hate communication, period.

(Ironic enough?)

It had been a long time since we spoke. She was one

of those friends, the kind who disappear on you as

soon as they enter a relationship. I guess she had

been going through some tough waters because that's

the only time she would call me.

We did the casual talk and then we talked about

what she called me for, obviously.

"I don't understand how you can spend so much time

with someone,

and then in an instant, they are gone," she said.

"That's life. People come and go."

"I just don't feel the same anymore,

and now I feel more trapped within myself . . .

more than ever, more than before."

Her voice trembled as if it was her last

word.

"Because some people can do that to you, kid. Some

people can free you from yourself," I said.

Soon after we hung up and I replayed those two

sentences over and over . . .

"They say when someone leaves, something inside of

you dies, but

they also say something inside of you is born."

Like a windmill caught in a hurricane, those words

kept cycling and cycling all over my head, over and

over with no bounds of no end . . .

And I am still trapped within myself, but I still

think

those were the wisest words I have ever heard.

Rebel Again

If you must rebel,

then rebel for a cause.

Do not riot into the night

for nothing.

If you must,

do it for change.

Do it for people.

Do it for all the things

that might kill you.

But above all,

do it for life.

It is all worth more

when you do it for life.

I Forgive You, My Love

And I forgive you for everything

you did not do.

It was not your fault.

You did not know how to be good,

how to love.

You did not know anything

about people or the way they

carried themselves

when they were hurt.

I forgive you.

I forgive you for leaving

when I needed you the most.

And now, in the aftermath,

I cannot even understand

my own language.

I do not know where I am

and I do not know who I have become.

And I just want to find myself

where I least expect it . . .

in the middle of my smile,

where my inspiration dwells.

No One Cares

But no one cares

and when they do

they want to make it seem

like it is all about you.

But their agenda is different

and it is always different.

It can be about money,

about fame,

about getting ahead,

but the similarity is

it doesn't concern you.

And you might think,

maybe they do care about me.

Maybe they do want to help me.

But in the end, it is mostly

all the same.

People want to use you.

So I feel you, Mr. Dylan,

when you say the times they are a-changin'.

Yes, they are changing and no

one gives a damn about anything

other than themselves.

Last Choice

If it is not you

then I want no one,

in this life and in the next.

You would be my first

and my last choice.

I love you

and I want you like a man

who has nothing:

in little daydreams,

in light whispers,

every day,

all the time.

There are times when words cannot
explain how I feel and that is
okay. Either way, thank you for
understanding my silence.

Becoming

And then

you became that place

I couldn't visit anymore.

That song

I couldn't listen to.

That memory

I couldn't relive.

That one night

I couldn't go back to.

You became everything

I wish I had.

Changing Matters

And now it is all different.

It has all changed

and she was more,

and there was more to her

than her fire.

Wild in love in all her

drunken glory . . .

She was everything I wanted.

She the ocean,

the sunset,

and all the best parts I fell into.

She was everything that

had ever made me feel

a little more.

She Has Too Much

"The girl has too much attitude.

Stay away from her," they say.

"She's trouble. Hard to love, hard to understand,

hard to control and run with."

Hell, they can make any woman look like a nightmare

but those bastards

have it all wrong.

Women like that, the ones with too much fire

inside, need something else and it is not something

you can find in stores. They need a little bit more

than that.

A little more soul,

a little more truth,

and above all, a little more love.

Broken Lightbulbs

I want to live in a place

where love isn't a metaphor for sex and silence

isn't a metaphor for fear. Where if you are

laughing all day, you're not considered crazy, and

if you want to actually help someone, it's not to

expect something in return. Where small talk

doesn't exist and people genuinely care. And where

you and I are closer together.

Imagine what a beautiful thing it can be. I want to

go there. I want to grow old there and above all, I

want to love there.

Scarecrows and Clouds

Life is frightening. Of course, anyone can tell you that, but more frightening than life itself is not knowing how it would turn out.

Like the you from five years ago would tell the you of today, "Well, that's odd. I didn't expect that to happen." And that's okay, because nothing goes the way you picture it. Nothing is ever really planned. Life is full of surprises, even when you expect something to happen.

Don't Ask Me

Don't ask me to leave because I might stay.

Don't ask me to stay because I might leave.

No one ever wants to be told how to live.

People don't work that way,

never have and never will.

So if I say I want you,

it doesn't mean I expect you to want me back.

That's not how it works.

If you want something you have to earn it.

You have to risk everything

for all the things you want to keep.

I rise like a flower from the
depths of my soul. I grow, I grow,
and all I do is wave at the people
as they come and go.

I Am a Diamond

You didn't destroy me.

I'm still here.

I'm still laughing and dancing

and getting myself back together.

You see, you didn't break me.

I broke myself

and most people have this terrible misunderstanding

of what hurts.

You see, if I loved you,

that's because I fell into it,

not because you pushed me off the edge.

I jumped.

I fell.

I got hurt.

Me. Me. Me.

And right now it's all about me.

So I'm sorry you came all this way to apologize.

I don't need that, and I'm sorry you came all this

way for nothing.

Make You Sad

I do not want to make you sad or make you cry.

No, never that.

I want to make you remember, make you realize.

I want you to take in life, all of it, completely.

I want you to acknowledge terrible things

and beautiful things

and how not all good is good

and not all bad is bad. That's all I want.

I want you to believe in yourself

and not panic if something goes wrong,

because some hearts do get broken

and some hearts never fully heal and sometimes

there are no happy endings, and that's okay.

You'll get through it.

You're strong enough. I know it.

I did not leave because of
you. I left because of me. I had
to go and yes, I do miss you
and I do love you but I love
myself more than anyone else,
and I deserve to work on myself
alone. Either way, I hope
you find what you are looking
for.

The Girl in the Bookstore

It's as if she contradicts herself.

She wants it all

but she doesn't know what to do with it.

She wants the day but she is far too in love with

the night.

She wants to understand herself

but she doesn't know where to begin.

And then I thought . . . how everyone was like

this.

No one really knew what they wanted

and when they did they want more.

We are all the same person after all.

Sunset

And there she goes,

walking as if she's dragging

the sun beneath her feet.

She goes, as she splits the atoms:

the ones of men and the ones of gods.

She doesn't break.

She consumes and then planets are born.

She is all things that are not here,

everything we see

but everything we could never

understand.

Everything Is Every Thing

Every door leads somewhere.

Every chance is a blessing.

Every song, every movie,

and every book is another world.

Every person you meet will

change your direction.

Every person you love will

strengthen your connection.

(The one to yourself.)

Every moment you spend looking,

something breathtaking will be

found. And above all,

every time you feel broken,

someone will be there

to help you heal.

You have to hope for all of these

and believe in them . . .

so you can learn to live better.

This is how you will find paradise.

STOP! You have less than five seconds
to think of someone, pick up your
phone, and tell them you love them.
Do it now, every second is a mystery.

All Broken Flowers Grow

I want to see you grow.

I want to see you for who you are.

I want ten years to pass,

so you could come back

and tell me how much you've loved,

how much you've learned.

I want to see you inspired

and touched by the flames inside you.

I want to see you do all the things we both know

you're capable of . . .

But I can't help you

if you can't help yourself,

because I believe in all the things that

move inside you.

So give yourself a chance

and I will be here

just in case you ever fall.

Boundaries

"I'm tired of living with boundaries.

I need to know what these wings can do. I need to

find out. Maybe my calling is out there," she said,

as they sat on the edge of the building watching

the city from above.

"No, sweet little love. Your genius. Your beauty.

Your struggle. Your art. Everything you'll ever

need isn't out there. Everything is in you. Believe

in yourself. Fall within yourself. That's where

you'll fly. That's where you'll expand your wings."

The Return

And sometimes

the one who left you broken returns.

And sometimes

they are different and sometimes

they show you how much they've changed.

And that alone might be one of the greatest

things in the world . . .

to have someone you once cared about

go through the trouble of finding you,

just to tell you

how much they still care.

We live in a bubble of fear, of
comfort, and all we do is complain of
the things we do not have, of the
things we cannot touch, and I cannot
break free without you. I need you.

Falling

You fall and break

because you are soft and fragile.

You fall and break

because you have too much inside you,

too much love and too much feeling,

and it is enough to cure the hatred in the world.

You fall and break

for the people you care about

and sometimes the ones you barely even know.

You fall and break

because sometimes you just have to

and because sometimes it is the right thing to do.

So keep falling and keep breaking,

little bird. It is, after all,

what makes you beautiful.

It is, after all, what makes you who you are.

And to be honest, I have never been more attracted

to anyone in my life.

I think I need you and I think you need me.

The Last Sentence

This is the last thing I want to tell you.

I want you to put yourself first,

no matter who you fall in love with.

I want you to love yourself

like it's the only thing left to do.

And lastly,

I want you to find someone

that will help you realize how important the first

two things are.

Your life should consist of making yourself happy

before giving your laughter away to

someone else.

Just Because

Because deep down inside you,

the sun rises and the moon sets.

Because deep down inside you,

there's more than what most people see:

an ocean deep enough to drown the world.

Because deep down inside you, there's a love

and it's connected to the way the planets move.

Because deep down inside you,

there's fire and snow,

life and death, strength and weakness,

and they're all fighting for your attention.

Because deep down inside you,

such places do exist and all places need to be

found, and they're all in you,

all you have to do . . .

is believe.

Birds

"She became everything that was around me.

She became these places, ones I knew existed but I

had never gone to. She became everything I wasn't

and everything I was."

"Then why did you let her go?"

"I didn't let her go. I set her free. She's like a

bird, and all wild birds should be free. Keeping

her caged would have killed her."

Strange things happen when I am alone. I think of you and I fall. I think of you and I ache. I think of you and I fly. Most days, I feel alone and sometimes I feel invincible.

Complicated Things

I am only interested in complicated things.

So do not give me what is easy,

that I do not want.

Give me the things you do not understand.

Give me the oceans you are too afraid to swim in,

and the trees you cannot climb

because they scare you.

Give me all the parts of you that you are afraid

of.

Give me what worries you,

what tears you apart.

If you are broken, then I will mend you.

I will dance with your fears

and make love to everything that makes you feel

alone.

Face the World

You should go out

and face the world as you once did

when you were young.

See the sky in different shades

and the trees for more than what they are.

You should stand beneath the rain

and feel more than little droplets of water

rushing through your skin.

You should wrap everything with your imagination,

by that I mean people and places,

and find the inspiration to make things better.

This is how we will survive.

This is how we will wander away,

but ultimately find each other again.

I have seen the world and I cannot
seem to wonder how none of those
places matter because you are not
here.

I Used to Love You

And I loved you

for the way you wrote music on my skin.

And you loved me

for the way I played the strings on your hair,

and together we made love in such a way

that artists do

when they create their works of art.

But in the end, none of that mattered,

for you were just another music lover,

and I

was just another one of your songs.

One Day

One day,

you will realize how there are some people

who are not meant to be yours.

One day,

you will have to move on,

and sometimes the most important thing to do

is to let go.

Think Too Much

You think too much

of all the things you want,

so you have forgotten

what it is you need.

And you don't need much, kid.

You just need a few good people,

and very few will carry love in their hearts.

So please,

stop overthinking.

Stop chasing the wrong things.

Listen to your friends.

Listen to the ones who love you

and understand how things change,

but the love they have for you

will always remain.

Dear friend, as you fall and as you break, I cannot help but to collect your pieces. You are beautiful and I will make you whole again.

Drunk One Night Prose

Everyone needs someone to hold on to,

and I'm glad you exist,

for without you

I could never imagine

what this world would be like.

Thank you. Thank you. Thank you.

Without you, I am nothing.

Matters of the Heart

One of the hardest things

to do in the world is . . .

to convince our minds

the doings of our hearts,

and trying to explain

to one another

why the other exists.

Another Night Drunk Prose

To all the artists who have influenced me,

I love you

although we will probably never meet.

I just want you to know how your music,

your poetry, and your art

has saved my life

and how it has made me feel less alone.

Thank you for all that you do.

Thank you for saving me.

And thank you for making my life

a little more than what it is.

It Is Always Okay

It's okay to feel alone,

lost, and empty.

For everything that's lonely

finds its company.

Everything lost is meant to be found

and everything empty eventually gets filled.

So see it like this:

Think about all the terrible times you have lived

through, and think about how they,

too, have passed.

You're a survivor

and you have to go through hell to find heaven.

The same way you must break in order to find

yourself whole again.

Legend

But greatness is usually frowned upon and ignored.

But the secret is to keep building.

No one is going to pay attention at first,

but if you keep going,

eventually someone will notice.

But you should never do it for other people.

Do it for yourself.

Build it for yourself and your future.

No one ever cares about the brick,

but everyone will stop

and marvel at the giant wall.

I keep coming back to the ocean
and I think it is because you felt
free there. I am your breeze and
you are my ocean and together we
will always be dreams to those who
are willing to look.

Feel Too Much Part 2

It hurts because you feel too much,

because you care too much,

and because you feel connected

no matter how far you go.

So to be honest, it will always hurt,

and you will go through life thinking

it is such a terrible thing.

But, my dear,

it is not, and I want you to keep feeling,

keep caring,

and keep loving,

for all those things do bring pain.

But I assure you, it is all quite worth it.

In other words, I need you to be you

when I need you most.

Be Gentle

Be gentle and kind.

Be fragile and soft.

I know the world tells you otherwise,

but deep down inside

you are not what they want you to be.

You are all things that change . . .

all leaves that fall,

all rain that meets the ground,

and all petals that the flower

can no longer hold.

So if you are meant to shatter,

then go ahead, break beautifully,

for the more you fall,

the more you rise and the more you do both,

the easier it will be to

find yourself again.

Things Happen

Things happen.

No one likes sudden movement.

No one wants to be pushed off the edge

while they're not ready to fly.

People get stirred.

People get forced into certain situations

and when they do, they change.

No matter how far they run, they change!

You'll change.

I'll change

and sooner or later we'll be different.

The world will be different

but the love we have for each other

will always be the same.

Come away with me and I promise
you, you will never feel the
burn of pain ever again.

Memory is a funny little thing.
It can give you all the pleasure
in the world or it can give you
all the ache it has to offer.
There is no in-between. That is
life and sometimes that is love.

Sadness

And it is sad how people come and go.

It is almost too beautiful to bear,

the way people gently come into our lives

to leave just as softly.

But that's life, right?

We make memories with other people

to remember them once they're gone.

We exchange experiences and expect to learn

something valuable in between.

The same way we have to learn to let go

and the same way we have to learn

how to embrace change as it comes.

And that's what makes this life beautiful,

for it is the coming and the going that makes us

who we are.

Feeling Lost Prose

We hurt ourselves

by loving other people

and I think we're all okay

with a little pain.

Feeling Lost Prose Part 2

The right person

can make you remember

or forget—all the moments

that took your breath away.

We come and we go but none of us
have the courage to stay.

Don't Sink

You don't have to sink to the bottom of the ocean

and watch the world as you fall.

You don't have to isolate yourself

because you're hurt.

People who love you will always be waiting

near the shore and every once in a while

it's okay to come to the surface to breathe.

We all need air to grow.

We all need an ocean to let go,

but it's people who will save you.

Always remember that.

Manufacturing Love

The things I want

cannot be bought or made in large quantities.

The things I want

are simple and do not worry the heart.

The things I want

can only be given once in a lifetime

and at any given moment.

And it is not love,

no it is not that!

I want laughter, freedom, and self-expression.

I want all the art that defines me.

All the things that hit me hard enough to move me

in such ways

the world has never seen.

This Woman

And that was the problem.

I wanted to get away.

I wanted to be as far away as possible.

That was the only way I could have understood you

and I didn't want to leave

but I did it anyway.

And to be honest,

I did it to feel closer to you.

So I could come back to give you

the love you deserved.

What She Said to Me One Night

I have too much universe in me.

I deserve more than the sky

and a few stars.

People Are Liars

People are liars.

They say strong hearts do not break,

wild hearts can be controlled,

and heavy hearts remain on the ground.

Well, this I say to you.

The strongest hearts do shatter,

the wildest hearts do roam free,

and the heaviest hearts do fly

and never come down.

So next time, please don't listen to other people.

So many are full of shit.

Break if you must,

find freedom because you need it to grow,

and fly beyond the imagination.

You must find yourself, love yourself, before

finding others like you who understand.

No More Love Please

You say you will not love again,

how your last relationship really destroyed you

and how love doesn't exist anymore.

Well, I say you're a liar,

for you will learn to love again

and every time you do,

it will hurt a little more than the last.

I just hope you find it when you least expect it.

The best kind of lovers are the ones who arrive

without a proper invitation.

Eventually it all hurts and yes,
I know things do get better, but
the days between now and then
are the hardest to come by. I
just hope I could survive another
storm until the sun comes back
into my life.

Breaking Atoms

We break because we are fragile.

We cry because what's inside

is too much to bear.

We hurt because the pain

doesn't know where else to go and we feel

because other people feel

and that's how we know we're connected.

And we search through life looking

for others like us, for the ones who

break, cry, and hurt.

And we feel them, we love them, and grow with them,

and together,

if we believe enough,

we will inspire the world

and learn how to make it beautiful again.

Sooner or Later

Sooner or later

you are going to find that place

you have been looking for

and it will pour there

and you will run beneath the rain

and stretch your arms there.

You will welcome the storm

and you will feel all the things

that stir inside you.

You will be happy there.

You will be free and you will find the inspiration

to love again.

Start to End

The same way it begins,

it ends,

and when it is over,

you realize how loving someone

and forgetting them is the same.

You realize

how night can sometimes be day

and how laughter can sometimes be tears.

You realize

so many things when someone is gone.

You realize

who you are and how much love you have given

to those who do not deserve it.

And to be honest,

in the end,

there is nothing worse to realize,

other than that.

Time Heals

Give yourself the time to heal.

It is okay to get your heart broken.

It is okay to shatter

and slip through the cracks a few times.

For the world wants you to believe

that loving yourself is an illness

but none of that is true.

Take the time to love yourself.

Your body isn't broken.

Your body is marvelous

and you are more than what they expect you to be.

You are everything they could never understand:

love and light mixed together

and all things that blow with the wind.

Openness

I don't know much about this world

but I do know one thing.

When people open their hearts

they find the courage to do remarkable things.

So keep your heart open.

I wouldn't worry about anything else.

Believe me, I know how you feel
and I know what it is like to have
the whole damn world against you,
watching you, hoping one day you
would fall, but you cannot fall.
You are stronger than that. I
believe it and so should you.

Find Her

And she did find her pieces in other people,

because ultimately,

that's what she would look for.

She found her smile

in a small boy in San Francisco.

She found her laughter

watching a couple in the middle of Chicago.

She found her dreams

listening to music one night in New York City.

And she never stopped finding new things about

herself.

She went on and became more.

She became whole and she was happy

and for the rest of her life

she found the inspiration she needed

to become the type of woman she had always

dreamed of.

Walk Away

And we should be together.

And my mind can't agree

with my heart. And my heart

is filled with endings, ones

without beginnings. And it

stings when I think about it.

And the slightest thought

sets me off. And I feel sad

but this is not a sad letter.

And my heart is an instrument,

a symphony of feelings

too beautiful to bear.

What I'm trying to say is,

I can't remember anything else,

other than the moment

you walked away.

Connected to You

I want to feel connected to you.

I want a string to be tied

from your heart to mine,

so we don't lose each other in the transition.

I've lost too many people,

too many feelings,

and too many things that have taken

my breath away.

I've been that person,

the one who's been taken for granted

one too many times

and I've suffered enough because of it.

I just want to know if this is real,

if we're real,

and if everything around us

brings us closer together.

That's all I want and I think everyone wants that.

I think everyone needs someone

to remind them

how to fall in love with themselves.

Midnight Prose Again

Maybe something good will come out of this

and it will be something I was meant for . . .

like tasting the stars on your lips

and watching the flowers bloom out of your skin.

I'm ready and I love you.

Live

When things break they never feel the same

and that's what made

whatever it was we had—sad.

We lasted

but not long enough.

We were close but not close enough.

And when it was over,

it was hard to be anything else,

when you were nothing more than just another

experience and I was just another person

who lived through it all.

The view from up here is beautiful.
I could see it all, from the
look in your eyes to the way
your mouth moves. I want to kiss
you. I never want to come back
down again.

Strange Expression

And I found it strange

how the people who were in love

couldn't express their love

and the people who were hurt

were always hurt.

And then,

they would trade positions,

like an off-and-on switch

and avoided one another at all costs.

And it was even stranger how

I, too, was like this.

I was lost between love and pain

and at any given moment

I would stumble and fall in love

to get up and fall in pain.

And this happened all of the time.

I was a walking contradiction

and as time went on

I never knew where I was going to end up.

I never knew who I was going to become.

Something to Remember

Because I know

in the bottom of your heart

there's a crack

and that's how the warmth gets in.

And because of that,

you shouldn't worry.

Always remember,

no matter how dark it gets,

the light will always be

on your side.

It Was Never for You

And sometimes

you realize how some people

are too damn heavy.

How sometimes letting go

is the only option

and how sometimes

the only way we can learn to fly

is if we stop chasing

the people

who were never meant for us

at all.

I drop my eyes on the sky and let the wind carry me home. I let my sadness become my wall and I protect my love with my solitude. You have to feel what I feel to understand me and once you do, you realize I am just like you.

Keep Going

There will always be

battles between the mind and the heart.

Between

the things you know

and the things you feel.

Between

what you want and what you need.

Between

who you are and who you want to be.

So remember, tomorrow is a new day and you will

always have a chance to succeed.

Keep going and stay strong.

You Have It in You

Miracles are happening inside you

and every day they are waiting

on the edge of the earth to change people's lives.

All you have to do

is give yourself a chance.

You have all the fires

and all the winds

to make this world a better place.

The Message I Left Her

Maybe something good will come out of this,

something I was meant for,

like tasting the stars on your lips

and watching the flowers bloom out of your hair.

I love you.

Fix You

The person who broke your heart

will not fix you,

the person who left you

will not come back to save you,

and the person who put you down

will not lift you into the air.

Now what you make of all three is up to you,

but it is always recommended

to ask them to go fuck off,

politely and kindly if necessary.

I am not sure what to feel about
anything anymore. I am not even
sure who I am, but when I am with
you, everything makes sense and
I feel more like myself than I
have ever been.

Back Together to Fall Apart

You will never stop putting yourself back together.

You will never stop breaking

and you will never stop pouring yourself

into all the things you love.

You will never stop, never,

because you are gentle, beautiful,

and delicate.

Because all human life is fragile

and all human life should be handled with care.

So slowly shatter into the earth,

softly pour yourself into the ocean,

and quietly pile yourself back together again.

Doing so is what makes the light in you something

worth stopping for

and every time I do,

you take my breath away.

And I appreciate that.

Drink to the Art

Because sometimes that movie,

that song,

and that painting say more about you

than you can about yourself.

Because sometimes that book

has your story and because sometimes

you have to believe in others.

That's the power of art.

We use it to communicate with others.

We use it to feel less alone.

She Left

And when she's gone . . .

I hope people remember her

for all the little things she left

behind. For the art she

made while she was being

herself and for the way she

inspired people to love

all over again.

Somewhere in the vastness of the earth, there is a place where people go to, to laugh. Where sadness is not allowed and only love is shared. This place is quiet and empty. This place beats 70 times per minute and the sound it makes is only for you. Come find me.

Too Beautiful for Words

You should let others see the goodness in you.

It's too damn beautiful to ignore.

You should let it out.

Let it pour.

I know it's hard to be judged.

I know hateful people,

people who have not yet found themselves,

make it hard for others to live,

and I know sad people don't stay sad forever.

So listen to yourself . . .

love yourself a little more.

You deserve to.

Don't waste your time in things that empty you.

Save yourself.

Only you can do that.

Pay Attention

And if you pay close attention . . .

you will find the gentle poetry in all places:

between all the things that make me miss you

and all the things that make me fall for you,

all over again.

Changing Directions

And there were times

when she felt lost.

But that did not stop her,

for the farther she went,

the more she collected herself

as she walked away,

and the more she walked away

the closer she got to it all.

In the end,

she became more than what she expected.

She became the journey,

and like all journeys,

she did not end.

She just simply changed directions

and kept going.

The Time Walks with You

But it is the smallest things

you miss when you lose someone.

Like the last kiss you shared

and the last time you looked into their eyes.

Those are the things that kill you.

Those are the things you take with you

as time goes by.

You are the only person I think of
when I am alone near the shore, and
I wish you could be here. I have
so much I want to share with you.

Lose It All

We all have to lose our minds a little.

We all have to follow our hearts blindly

and we all have to walk through the fire

no matter how bad it gets.

That is how you will find the things you need

to believe again.

That is how you will find your way

back home.

What Friends Do

It's okay to collapse into my arms.

You don't always have to be strong.

You don't always have to fight.

I am here,

and believe me when I tell you,

I have your back

and I will protect you till the very end.

Beautiful Girl

Beautiful girl,

the peace you've been searching for

can be found in your heart.

So let it ache, let it fall,

for underneath those untamed forces

you will find your love.

Your ultimate silence,

a truth the world will always be

too afraid to hear.

Broken Wings

But leaving is an art,

and I have painted enough

birds with broken wings . . .

And I have watched them go

into the horizon, for they

have learned how to fly again

and I have learned how to

let them go.

Time moves strangely when you are in love and sometimes when I am with you, I forget where I am.

Beautiful Chaos

She's so beautiful,

you could almost feel the sun breaking around her

as she walks into a daydream . . .

like a runaway child

and she exhales devastation

like the last time you said her name.

Small Fires Start Bigger Fires

She loves out of mind,

out of what hurts . . .

and that's why she wants to save you,

because deep down she's the type of woman

who wants to fix broken things . . .

So to be with her

you must understand,

how her heart is strong enough to heal the world.

Home Again

I woke up feeling everything again.

I woke up remembering

how it all began and how it all ended . . .

and I thought

how maybe love was a lot like this.

How maybe

one day I would be able to wake up

in your heart

and learn to call it home again.

The Reveal

There is life in the moment

right before a kiss,

and some will argue it is poetry

but I believe it is more.

I believe it is our hearts revealing secrets

our lips could never reveal to each other

or to ourselves.

We are here. This is our generation and we are beat up and tired. We no longer believe in your rules and we came here to change your old ways. Do not fuck with us. We are not playing. We are here to take all the things that do not belong to you.

She Is Stars and Moons

And if there's a universe in her,

then by all means let it be free,

let it be born,

and let it carry this pain

within me out of my body.

Let it be worth more than a

thousand lovers

and a million I love yous.

Let her stars and moons

be my church and let

loving her be my only religion.

1999 Prose

And as you walked away,

I sat back and laughed

at the love

I was never meant to have.

Make Me Feel

They say a picture is worth a thousand words

and I can't seem to wonder

how you see a thousand different things

but none of them define

how you feel.

She Came Looking

And at times,

she didn't know many things.

She didn't know if she wanted to remain lost

or if she wanted someone to come looking for her.

She didn't know if she wanted to stay

or if she wanted to go.

She didn't know who she was

or who she was meant to be . . .

but she did know one thing.

She knew she wanted someone

to fall in love with her heartbeat

before they fell in love

with anything else she had to offer.

Kiss Kiss

And tonight we are together

and tonight is far more

perfect than the night before

and tonight we whisper

and tonight it is all about you

and tonight I think I love you more

and tonight the sky is full

of old literature

and tonight they all say the same thing.

"Kiss her well and make her

forget who she is."

Sometimes I do not have much to say, and I know I should tell you the way you make me feel but I will not. I'd rather show you. I'd rather prove my love than cover your heart with a collection of empty words.

The Cycle

And we can't let go

because we hold on

like it's never going to happen again,

but it does and it will.

It all repeats itself over

and over again.

Universe

Sometimes it's okay to be alone.

It's okay not to know or even care.

You don't always need someone.

You don't always need to know where you're going,

for you have loved

and cared far enough.

This time,

you should think about yourself . . .

love yourself,

be alone with yourself,

and do everything you need to do for yourself.

Believe . . .

and you will find the edge of the universe

within you.

Running Away

And all your life you thought

breaking free meant you were fighting to move

forward,

but in reality,

you were only walking farther away.

I present you a flower. It is filled
with my deepest memories. I want you
to have it. So please do not lose it.
If you do you will lose me forever.
Keep me and remember me whenever you
are sad.

I Wasn't Inspired

And as time passed

she felt better about herself

and her life.

She let herself go,

the same way lovers let go.

She knew things were about to change for the best.

And like all things that were worth it,

she took a chance,

and she did it without regret,

without hurt,

and without her guard up.

The Stars Are Not Too Far

And you will remain far yet near.

Like the wind rushing through our hair.

Like the reason distant stars

only appear in the dark.

And like all

things that come close

but not enough to make our own.

I Am with You

I don't know many things.

Like why people leave

and why things happen the way they do . . .

but I do know one thing.

I know how I feel when you say

I am yours

and I know who I am

when I am with you

and I wouldn't change a thing

about that.

Wine and Poems

Because there is nothing in her I would change,

for she is made of wine

and unfinished poems,

and her past tastes a lot like sadness

and winter rain . . .

and I love her at her best

and even harder at her worst.

She takes me to a reality that has never existed,

and sometimes,

I am lost beneath her rib cage

without looking for a way out.

We are not meant to be held forever. Therefore, you should catch me now before someone else does.

Open Your Eyes

All the lies you tell yourself

to get through the day,

then a new day arrives

and this is how you continue

to live your life . . .

and somehow you're okay with this.

You're okay with being other people

rather than yourself.

I Need You

And perhaps, one day,

we will learn the difference between

the want and the need of another person.

Perhaps, one day,

you will walk back into my life

because you need to

and not because I want you to stay.

Myself and Me

I'm good at breaking my own heart.

I'm good at piecing myself back together

and there's nothing you could do to destroy me.

So if it hurts . . .

it's only because I did this to myself

and I wouldn't have it any other way.

The Hardest Thing to Do

And as she walked away,

I finally understood

how sometimes the hardest thing to do

is to let another person

love you.

Prayers about You

But my heartaches grow

from all the places you have

touched

and now I am left with a garden

full of prayers

and they are all about you.

Maybe Who Knows

Maybe one day

we'll finally learn to love ourselves

and stop apologizing

for the things that make us

who we are.

When She Was Young

Her rib cage isn't built to harbor

so much pain,

and yet she walks into an ocean of darkness

and finds the inspiration

to burst into a billion stars.

Chaos

Somewhere within her,

maybe

in the marrow of her bones . . .

there are a thousand cities.

And yet

she speaks of chaos

as if she doesn't know

what lies beneath

her chest.

I Love You More

I know you're broken

and I don't say this just to say it,

but I know you've been through hell and back

and it has changed you.

You're not the same person I once knew

and it's not that I want to fix you

or save you

or anything that has to do with that.

It's more like

I will accept you

and take your flaws

for more than what they are.

If you're a hurricane

then I'll be the sea

that gives you the strength

to go on.

Writing on the Earth

I am not too afraid

to fall into the ocean

but every time I do

I think

how there would never be enough sand for me

to write about all the things

you make me feel.

Save Yourself

You don't need someone to save you.

Maybe what you need

is someone to teach you

how you are worth saving

and show you

how that is something only you can do

for yourself.

Roots from Broken Flowers

You can get yourself into certain situations

but I can assure you,

every time you overcome something

you won't be the same person . . .

and it's the same idea with every person you meet.

You cross paths,

exchange memories,

and from there on

you're someone else,

and how you grow from it

is entirely up to you.

The Things I Can't Tell Myself

I broke my own heart chasing you,

saving you, and loving you.

And I lost a lot of time doing so,

but this time

it's all about me.

So you can't come back demanding my attention.

That's not how this works.

You can't just make an entrance

when the door has been closed for so long.

People Like Us

You can't stop certain things from happening.

You have to stop trying to control everything.

Sometimes

you're going to lose.

Sometimes

you're going to be last.

The world wasn't built on perfection.

It was built day by day

and by people like us.

Fly Fly Fly

"I feel free with you," she said.

"Why?" he replied. His eyes scanned through the
room as if he were reading her feelings on the
wall.

"Because you inspire me and that alone might be the
most dangerous gift a person can present to
another. You give me the courage I need to get my
inner spirit going, and because of that I now
believe how you don't need a pair of wings to fly."

I Appreciate You

I know you feel as if you're not appreciated.

I know you've let so many people in,

thinking maybe this time it will work out,

maybe this time

I have found the one I'm supposed to live for.

I know every time someone leaves,

you lose a little more of your humanity,

you lose your hope.

I know all these things about you,

not because your eyes

have this tamed sadness within them,

but because I, too,

understand what it's like to love

and be unloved at the same time . . .

And I, too,

understand what it's like

to have a heart made of firewood.

I burn for the things I desire,

and like you,

all I really want is for someone

to fill my heart with adventure.

I will meet you on the other
side. Just promise me that you
will return back home.

Sea, Sand, and Skies

We are the same,

you and I.

We fall in love

with the stars that don't belong to us

instead of the ones

burning in our hands.

We fall in love

with the breaking instead of the healing.

We fall in love

with drowning instead of the sea.

And we fall in love

with our memories instead of our future.

Read This Every Day

How many people

do you have to fall in love with

until you finally understand

that the only person

you owe yourself to . . .

is you.

Afraid of What Is There

It's okay not to know

how to handle your own heart.

You should be afraid of it.

It roars,

it shifts,

it changes direction . . .

It does all these powerful things

and still,

it fits in one hand

and shatters the moment

the one you love lets it

slip away.

Too Hard to Understand

You lost her

and it wasn't because she was hard to hold,

or love,

or touch,

but because she was made of your absence,

of all the things you ignored

and all the beautiful poetry

you read but failed to understand.

Terrible Lives

Because some people

live these terribly confused lives.

They have it all backward.

They think love is the fear of abandonment.

They think love is attachment

and what is worse is,

they think love is forcing someone

to stay.

Bloom

You don't need

someone's attention to feel important.

You bloom off the top of your eyes.

Open them.

See the possibility.

The world is far more inspiring

when you see it

for the first time.

For So Long

And one day,

you will understand

how some people feel familiar

the moment you meet them . . .

as if your souls have met many years ago

and they pick up

right where they left off.

And one day,

out of the blue,

someone will run up to you

and tell you . . .

"I have been waiting for you

and I have missed you for so long."

Anyone Else Is Not for Me

I know there are other people out there

I could possibly fall in love with

and I know

how I might have a better shot of happiness

but what's the point?

I found you

and you speak to me in ways I can't imagine,

and because of that

I don't care about anyone else

other than you.

Sad Eyes

I know you're hiding something

behind those sad eyes.

You're afraid to show your soul

but I'm telling you to trust me.

Trust me with every atom that holds you together.

I want to know the real you,

the you that knows silence,

abandonment, and pain.

The you the world isn't ready for.

Life is hard as it is.

There is no reason to make loving you

even harder.

If you move too fast you will miss the point. You will miss the little things, and I need you to remember me before I go.

Sometimes

I can't apologize for who I am,

but I can apologize for the things I do

and I can't love you without hurting you.

The same way

I can't hold on to your heart

without letting it slip through my hands.

Sometimes I break the things I love

and sometimes the things I love break me.

Scars Are Made of Gold

They're scars for a reason.

They don't hurt anymore

but they're there to remind you

of all the things you lived through.

The moments that almost killed you

and the ones that made you

who you are.

Stay strong.

Broken People

I like broken people

with broken eyes and broken smiles.

I like people who feel too much

and have seen even more.

I like people who are silent

because they appreciate how sometimes

words can't explain the moment.

I like people who find themselves

in the most unusual places—where they go

to fall apart in solitude.

I admire these people,

I look up to these people,

and I appreciate these people,

for they know more about true love

than anyone else.

Grow in the Darkness

You have to allow yourself to break apart.

That's the only way you're going to know

what you're made of.

Let yourself go.

Let yourself fall.

Let yourself drown.

Let yourself shatter.

And above all,

let yourself get hurt.

Do all these things and know . . .

How you have to really know your demons

to defeat them.

Befriend them to destroy them.

Love them and walk with them.

That's the only way you're going to bloom.

Why I Miss You, My Brother

Because the end of the world happens

at least once every hour

since you've been gone.

Because all the things I've told you

I've really meant.

Because without you there is no me.

Because it hurts

but I'm still breathing.

Because they say "letting go" will "help me"

but all I could do is think about you.

Because I still love you

and you are not here.

It's No Longer Here

I cannot remember the ocean.

I live near it

and yet,

I cannot remember it.

It is not because I cannot go to it

but rather

because I choose to ignore it

because I know it is always there.

If I go far, the ocean stays.

If I die, the ocean stays

but somehow I cannot remember it.

The same way I cannot remember many things,

like things I used to do when I was a kid.

Things that fed my soul.

I cannot remember things.

Sometimes I don't know myself.

Sometimes I can't remember who I am.

The same way I can't remember you.

I can't.

Maybe this prose isn't making any sense

but that is not the point.

If you read this

and don't get it

then you just missed the point.

I cannot remember the ocean.

I cannot remember who I used to be.

Selective Programming

There are hidden truths in films,

music, and in stories.

Some truths cut deeper than others

and some truths are too ridiculous to even

consider.

There are hidden truths in media.

What you see is either fact or fiction

but most fiction is fact.

It is just buried from the population.

Fifty years before the moon landing, critics and

the people said it was impossible. They made films

about it, wrote music about it, and even stories.

Now people walk on the moon.

Selective programming.

I want you to see things the way I see.

If I tell you man can fly it is because man can

fly. I see it before it has happened.

If they tell you aliens exist it is because they do

and when they reveal themselves, you will be okay

with it.

Selective programming.

Here are the things that are on the media now:

wars, invasions, laser weapons, reptilian gods,

flying pyramids, and upside-down crosses.

Kind of makes you want to think of all the things

you might see tomorrow.

Selective programming.

You were happy once. You were cheerful and full of laughter. That is how I want to remember you. You are beautiful and I miss you.

People Killer

The cops just killed an innocent man.

He wasn't doing anything wrong.

He was black and the cop was white.

I can't understand this racism thing.

This authority thing.

Cops are the law.

The law controls us all.

For every one cop there are ten thousand of us.

Cops can kill you for no reason

but you can go straight to jail, to hell, the

moment you kill, and for whatever reason.

Maybe someone broke into your house,

kidnapped your kid or even your mother.

You can't kill to protect yourself but a cop can

kill for pleasure.

I saw the cops kill an innocent man.

The video showed the man on the ground

surrendering. It took five shots, the black man is

dead. The cop said he had a gun.

There was no gun.

When the people kill each other, it's your word

against theirs.

A cop kills a man and he's off the hook.

I saw a cop kill an innocent man.

His family mourns his death

while the cop sits at home and enjoys his meal.

This Is My Space

What a suicide it is,

this social media stream.

This endless ocean of moments.

Once hooked it is over.

Once you are a member

it is as if you have signed

a life contract.

This prison.

This system.

This, this and that, that.

We all get on daily.

In the morning,

in the afternoon,

and in the very second

before we go to bed.

This social media thing is

in the blood.

It gives us life,

excitement, and something to look forward to.

But what to do if no one stimulates you anymore.

That is,

if no one replies or sends you messages.

What becomes of this social pool

if no one appreciates you or comes looking for you.

If no one cares about your moments, your pictures,

or even your videos.

What becomes of your social media if you die. Does

it die with you?

Perhaps it does, the same way

lovers die out into flame,

the one that no longer keeps us warm.

If there is no reaction then there is no action, no

purpose to keep it going.

It is the need of human interaction

that keeps us all online.

Dear Mother

Dear Mother,

If I die,

do not let me become a hashtag.

I am so much more than a few letters.

I am so much more than what I am.

Within me I have answers,

I have questions,

I have love,

and I have hatred.

All these twirl within me.

Aching my body for a sudden way out.

Dear Mother,

If I die,

do not let me become a hashtag.

Hashtags die down, they don't last.

They come and they go.

And I want to stay in people's hearts

the same way our childhood has stayed in ours.

Dear Mother,

If I die,

do not let me become a hashtag.

I know there is more to people than sharing

terrible news and talking about how cops have

murdered innocent African-Americans.

I know there is a light in every one of us

and I know we all want change but do not know how

to touch change.

Dear Mother,

If I die,

just promise me this:

Do not let me become a hashtag.

There are so many other things I can become.

I know it.

To Charise:

May your flame live
within me,
and continue to
inspire me
through every
waking hour.

I can feel you flowing in me.

With open eyes I see the world,
with an open heart I see the souls,
and with an open mind I see it all differently.

Thank you for your time.

Robert M. Drake

We will rebuild this world.

Follow R. M. Drake
for excerpts and updates.

Facebook.com/RMDRK
Twitter.com/RMDRK
Instagram.com/RMDRK
RMDRK.Tumblr.com

For Gui,

One day I will find you
and we will laugh
and it will be as if
we are seeing each other
for the very first time.

Rest easy my brother.